DEADLY MEMOS

HOW CONVENTIONAL WISDOM KILLS COMPANIES

Jeffrey Severts is the co-founder and executive director of the Center for RISC at the University of Chicago. He has spent most of his career in business, working as a C-level executive for large consumer brands in the food, consumer technology and retail sectors. His innovative approach to management issues has been featured in *The Wall Street Journal, The New York Times, The McKinsey Quarterly*, and Gary Hamel's, *The Future of Management.*

Deadly Memos

How Conventional Wisdom Kills Companies

Pamphlet #1: Performance Management

Jeffrey D. Severts

Copyright 2021 Jeffrey D. Severts
Cover design by Mara Severts
Cover copyright 2021 Jeffrey D. Severts

The scanning, uploading, and distribution of this pamphlet without permission is a theft of the author's intellectual property. If you would like permission to use material from the pamphlet (other than for review purposes), please contact jseverts@gmail.com.
Thank you for your support of author's rights.

First Edition: September 2021

Print book interior design by Mara Severts and Jeffrey D. Severts

ISBN: 9798467015705

To Ahna

CONTENTS

Introduction: A Framework for the Life Cycle of Companies   8
How a company's size affects its ability to grow... How profit growth deceives us... The four stages every successful company goes through... The Veil of Scale.

Pamphlet #1: Performance Management   24
What a 1984 performance review for Prince might have looked like... The four problems underlying all performance reviews... The only correct goal of performance management... Why you shouldn't link pay and performance... Why reviews should be voluntary... What the US Army can teach Walmart... How forced rankings help both Prince and Ray Parker Jr.... The only good use for committees.

INTRODUCTION

A Framework for the Life Cycle of Companies

We all know that most companies struggle as they get older and bigger. But why does this happen?

To some extent, we think we know the answer. We talk about organizations becoming slow and "bureaucratic," as if it is an inevitable, almost biological process. But do we really understand how this works? What are the mechanisms by which companies become less nimble, creative, and exceptional? And can anything be done about it?

I will try to answer these questions with this series of pamphlets. My hope: That a better understanding of what is really happening inside our organizations will give us a chance to fight off, or at least delay, bureaucratic death.

These pamphlets will be very unlike typical business books. As the word "pamphlet" suggests, I will keep them short and to the point--no windy anecdotes about what today's hot companies are doing, and no recycled arguments to appease some publisher's appetite for high page counts. I will also strive to keep things interesting, starting each pamphlet with a lighthearted, fictional memo to illustrate some of the more absurd parts of our corporate lives. And finally, I will try my best to avoid the buzzwords and cliches that infect the world of business.

At the end of each pamphlet, I will offer up some ideas for addressing the issues I have raised, focusing on practical changes you can experiment with in your own organization. I offer these not as perfect solutions, but as kernels of unconventional wisdom that might allow you to imagine new ways of doing things.

This first pamphlet will focus on performance management. But before we delve into that subject, it is important to establish a basic framework for how companies change as they grow.

A Corporate Life Cycle Framework

The argument that firms become more dysfunctional as they grow larger seems hard to square with the reality we see around us. We buy all our stuff from Amazon. We drink our coffee at Starbucks. And we scroll the day away on Apple products. Clearly some large companies are doing just fine.

Our lives are dominated by large firms because there are many advantages to being large. Big companies often have widely known brand names, lower costs, and even political influence that can help them to push aside their competitors.

But growth creates costs, too. Sometimes those costs are easy to see, and sometimes they are more insidious. Either way, they are always related to the unnatural condition of trying to coordinate the actions of thousands of people.

The framework that follows will illustrate how these competing forces affect the fortunes of companies in the different stages of their "lives." It will help explain the paradox of how big firms can both dominate the marketplace *and* suffer the crippling effects of being large.

The Framework

Companies, as collections of human beings, go through a life cycle I have illustrated in Figure 1. On the horizontal axis, I have located the size of a firm, with organizations moving to the right as they grow larger. On the vertical axis, I have placed the quality of a company's proposition. The red, roller-coaster-shaped curve on the graph is the minimum proposition performance required by a given company to maintain healthy, profitable growth at different stages of its life.

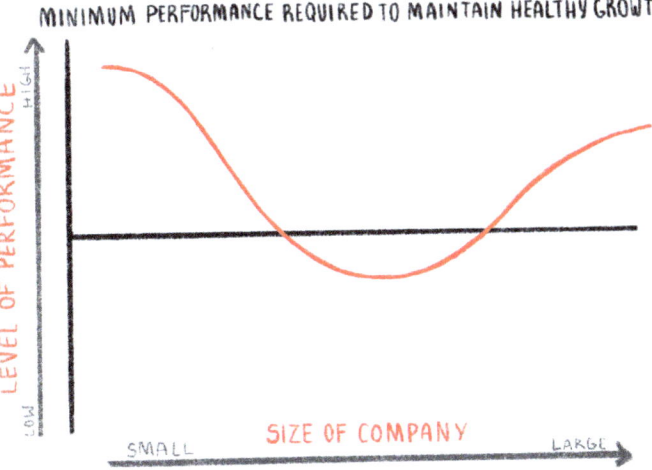

FIGURE 1

What is a proposition? Quite simply, the company's offering to its customers--the products and services that are meant to solve customers' problems.

What does "performance" mean? It refers to the strength of the proposition relative to alternatives in the market on dimensions that customers care about. It could be cost, quality, design, convenience, prestige . . . any number of things. Strong propositions will typically exceed all competitors on at least one of these dimensions without materially underperforming on the others. All other things being equal, a stronger proposition should win more market share, especially in the longer run.

So what should you notice about Figure 1? Most critically, that *the minimum performance required to keep a company growing at a healthy pace varies as the company grows.* When a company is small, it needs a very strong proposition to thrive. The same is true again when the firm is large. However, at a certain stage in a company's life, a stage I call the Veil of Scale, a firm can lag the market with its proposition and still do quite well.

This conclusion is profoundly different from what management teams, business school academics, and investment analysts believe. Their conventional wisdom is that a company's profit growth, regardless of what stage it is in, is the strongest indicator of the strength of its proposition and its longer-term health.

If only it were that simple.

Stage I: The Struggle to Get to Scale

In the first stage of a company's life, it faces tremendous disadvantages. It has very little money, only a few employees, and perhaps even fewer customers. To overcome these hurdles, a small firm needs a brilliant, differentiated proposition. This is easy to say but very hard to do. Only a tiny percentage of small companies ever develop something so special. The rest create propositions that are somewhere between really bad and pretty good, causing nearly all Stage I firms to remain small or die.

Really good propositions are difficult to create and even more challenging to keep alive. When an entrepreneur, after rubbing two sticks together for years, generates a glowing ember of an idea, she must carry it around with her, protecting it from all the forces that are trying to quench it. Those forces can be competitors, but they can also be regulators, poorly performing employees, or naysaying stakeholders. It is a formidable task, and her business is unlikely to survive. Half of all startups die within five years and over eighty percent disappear within another two decades.[1]

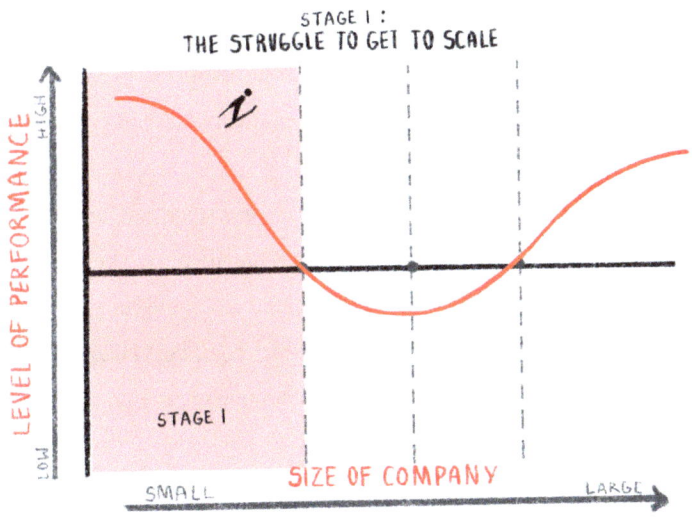

FIGURE 2

---

[1] https://www.bls.gov/bdm/us_age_naics_00_table7.txt; Bureau of Labor Statistics study referred to tracked 570,000 startups from 1994 - 2019.

If an entrepreneur somehow beats the odds and develops an amazing proposition, her company will start to enter an exciting phase of scale benefits. Everything begins to get easier as the company gets bigger. Chaos is reduced as processes are established. Tasks get simpler as systems come online. And as more employees are hired, some are able to specialize, allowing for further gains as they learn to do their jobs very well. At this point, the latter half of what I call Stage I, the company feels like it is flying (Figure 2.)

It is exciting to be in organizations that are living through this stage. Everyone is happy, optimistic, and infused with energy. Anything seems possible. People take risks, work hard, help each other, and persist in the face of setbacks. The company, to some extent, gets supercharged by its success, allowing the same group of employees to now accomplish more.[2]

It is important to note that companies in this stage can be surprised and quickly punched out by their competitors. The fast growth they are experiencing can make them feel immortal, but they are still relatively small and vulnerable. Their best insulation against a quick reversal of fortune is to continue to provide their customers with a brilliant proposition.

---

[2] This stage can sometimes be artificially created by a large infusion of investor capital, creating some of the same benefits but opening the company up to new risks as well. For recent examples of this, see WeWork and Uber.

Stage II: The Veil of Scale

In the second stage (Figure 3) of a company's life, as scale benefits continue to accumulate, nearly everything gets easier. A firm's size is now becoming an asset. It has talent, money and knowledge that give it clear advantages over smaller competitors.

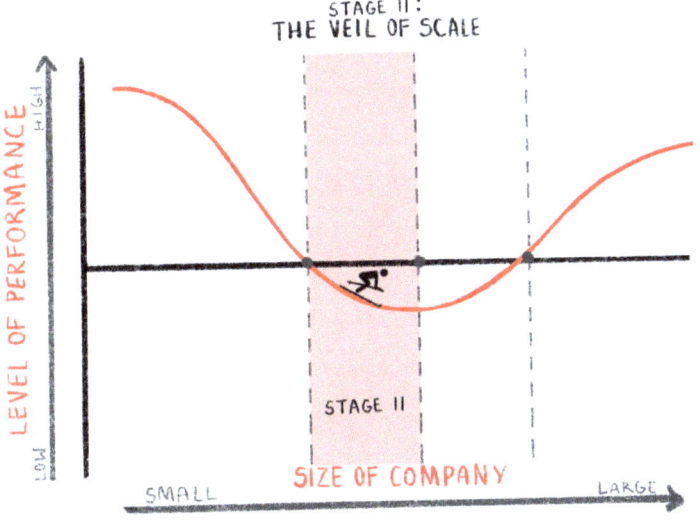

FIGURE 3

These advantages are so great, and making money is so much easier than it was in Stage I, that a company can get away with delivering a below-average proposition to the market and still continue to grow revenue and profits.

This is when the Veil of Scale descends on a company, causing a form of mass delusion. Employees feel the thrill of skiing downhill, with sales and profit targets whizzing past them at high speed, often not realizing that the gravitational push of scale is subsidizing their results. This is a dangerous time because organizations will deceive themselves into thinking their success is deserved. Employees within the firm start to confuse cause and effect, believing that their presence, their work, and their decisions are better than they are. Confidence and power start to accumulate, reducing the quality of decision-making.

To make matters worse, the financial rewards to employees are typically growing rapidly during this stage. Bonuses are big and consistent. Equity stakes, if they exist, are becoming very valuable. Things are really good, and people now have a lot to lose. This reduces the incentives to innovate and take risks, two critical inputs for creating value. *In short, the behaviors that created a company's success now become rarer and go unrewarded.*

Stage III: The Scale Flip

In the third stage (Figure 4) of a company's life, the "polarity" of scale flips. Instead of everything getting a bit easier, it now feels like a firm is trying to ski uphill. Financial targets grow harder to achieve each year, and everything a company needs to do requires more effort.

Why does this flip happen? Because, at this point, the benefits of being large have started to be outweighed by the costs. Decision rights are becoming unclear, with multiple groups expecting to advise or control every major initiative. Information is getting trapped in all the corners and crevices of the company, causing employees, especially those higher in the hierarchy, to make "stupid" (uninformed) decisions. And inertia is becoming the most formidable force--bad projects never die, good projects never get started, and the company's old strategy horse continues to get flogged, despite plentiful evidence that it can no longer run.

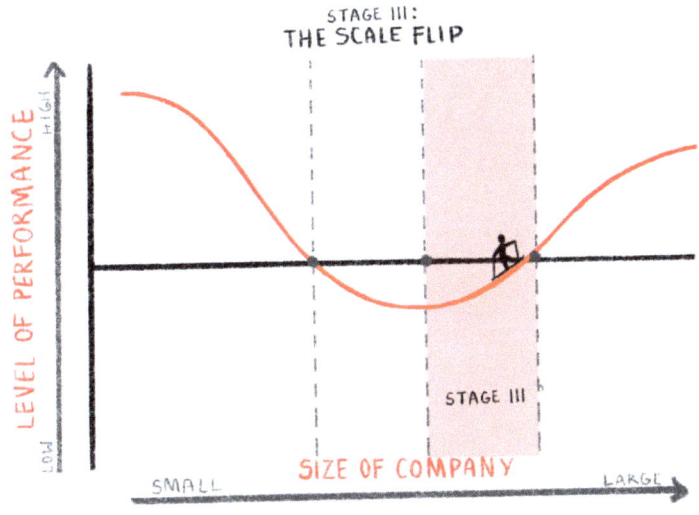

FIGURE 4

This extra friction inside the company makes everything harder, and it increases as the company grows. The only way to offset this burden is for the company to start improving its proposition to its customers, something it probably has not done since it was in Stage I.

Stage IV: The Scale Slog

In the fourth and final stage (Figure 5), the costs of scale are now painfully acute, overwhelming the benefits that size used to afford the firm.

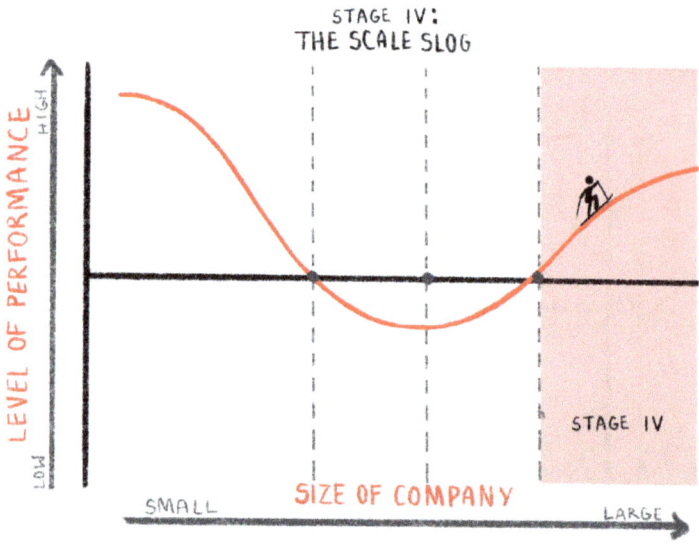

FIGURE 5

Getting anything done inside a Stage IV company is very difficult. The structural challenges that began to emerge in Stage III (e.g. unclear decision rights; poor information flows; inertia; etc.) are bad enough, but damage to the organization's spirit is often the bigger problem. Employees have not experienced success of any kind in a long time. They grow pessimistic and avoid taking risks. They stop dreaming and creating. And because they cannot see a path out of this mess, they start looking for ways to capture and preserve a larger share of the shrinking pie for themselves.

To overcome all this, a company must not only improve its proposition, but it must somehow get back to substantially outperforming its competition. *This is very hard to do, so most Stage IV firms eventually die--or become the living dead.*

"Very hard" is not the same as impossible, of course. Some large companies do manage to overcome the burdens of being big. Apple is probably the most prominent, recent example. Without reviewing the entire history of the company, something I am happy to leave to others, let me offer a simple map (Figure 6) of my view of the strength of Apple's proposition since its incorporation in 1977.

After its spectacular early success, Apple fell into a deep malaise in Stage II. This is very atypical, but Apple lost both Steve Jobs and Steve "Woz" Wozniak in this period, and was under intense pressure from Microsoft's Windows operating system, so it very quickly fell from having a world-beating proposition to presenting a confusing array of uncompetitive products.

In 1997, only weeks from bankruptcy, Apple's board brought back Steve Jobs in one final, desperate act. Flush with almost despotic powers, Jobs not only worked feverishly to hold off the costs of scale by simplifying the product line and removing resistant executives, but more importantly, he led the development of some of the most remarkable consumer products of our lifetimes.[3] This new proposition catapulted the company from below the line to far above it, fueling immense growth in its revenues, profits, and stock price.

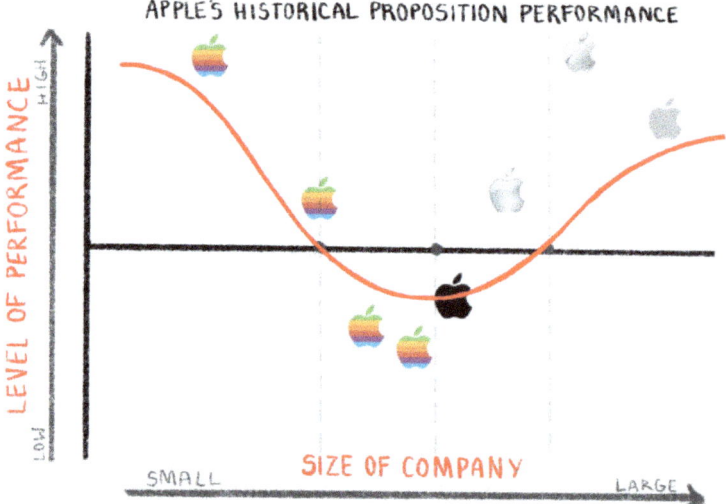

FIGURE 6

---

[3] Walter Isaacson, *Steve Jobs* (Simon & Schuster, 2011) and https://en.wikipedia.org/wiki/Apple_Inc.

Since Jobs' passing in 2011, Apple's product launches have been less spectacular. While the company's total proposition is still above average, it appears to have moved much closer to the line, leaving it vulnerable again to the costs of scale. Without a new, big improvement to its offering, Apple's long run of exceptional revenue and profit growth will likely end.

Can Apple or any other Stage IV company thrive without someone like Steve Jobs at the helm? Of course, but not without some radical breaks from the conventional corporate wisdom.

In Sum

The life cycle framework I have described here can be summarized as follows:

- In Stage I, when companies are small, they face immense disadvantages in the marketplace. The only way they can grow to be a large company is through a brilliant, market-beating proposition.
    - Such propositions are very rare, which is why so few small companies ever become large.
- In Stage II, the "Veil of Scale" descends on companies. As they grow larger, the advantages of scale start to accumulate, making it much easier for them to grow and make money.
    - This is the stage during which companies can deceive themselves (and outside observers) into thinking they

are doing better than they are. Revenues and profits may continue to flow in, even as their proposition slips from brilliance to mediocrity.
- In Stage III, the costs of scale that come with growth begin to completely offset the benefits, making it more and more difficult for large companies to grow profitably.
  - This series of pamphlets is dedicated to exploring these costs in detail.
- In Stage IV, the final stage, the costs of scale are painfully acute, overwhelming the benefits that size used to afford these companies.
  - The only way to create value as a Stage IV firm is to develop an extraordinary proposition. This is very hard to do, especially while burdened with the costs of being large.
  - Creating an amazing proposition in Stage IV is very hard, but it's not impossible. Today's thriving large companies have done it, but their position is perilous.

PAMPHLET #1

Performance Management

March 3, 1985

Warner Bros. Records
4000 Warner Blvd., Burbank, CA 91522

Dear Mr. Prince Rogers Nelson,

We have come to that dreaded time of year again—performance review season.

HR is changing the performance review template for the fourth time in four years, and the new version hasn't come in yet from the printer, so I am taking the liberty of substituting this letter for the official form.

You have had a solid year with us, Mr. Nelson. The Purple Rain *album and movie have done well, but I am sure you will agree that we all have opportunities for improvement. What follows is my assessment of your performance for fiscal year 1984.*

SUCCESS FACTORS

Job Skills and Knowledge: *You write, arrange, produce, sing all the vocals, and play all the instruments on your albums. And Eric Clapton says you are the greatest guitar player of all time--Eric Clapton, for Christ's sake! Still, I* *would like to see you teaching some of the younger members of the team more often. You have so much to share.* ***Score: (4/5)***

Teamwork: *While always polite to your fellow employees, we continue to be concerned about your aforementioned tendency to not involve other team members in the production of our albums. We are happy to see you have finally brought in* The Revolution *to back you up for* Purple Rain. *This is good progress, but we hope to see you continue to improve in this area.* ***Score: (2/5)***

Work Quality: Purple Rain *topped the Billboard album chart for 24 weeks. "When Doves Cry" and "Let's Go Crazy" both reached #1, "Purple Rain" hit #2, and "I Would Die 4 U" peaked at #8. We sold 1.5 million copies in the first week of release. Two Grammys. One Oscar.* ***Score: (4/5)***

Communication and Presence: *I don't know if you have heard this feedback before, but you are kind of a shy guy. You don't speak much in meetings, letting others overshadow you. We would all benefit from you asserting yourself more. Please bring some of that stage presence into the conference room!* ***Score: (3/5)***

Meets Deadlines: *I am sure I don't need to remind you that* *we barely made our target release date for* Purple Rain. *While I understand you were very busy with the tour and the movie preparations, you allowed these distractions to keep you from finishing all the tracks by the delivery dates outlined by the Project Management Team. Did you realize that Margie down in the mailroom had to use the express shipping option to get the promotional copies out to the stations on time? This was a costly mistake.* **Score: (2/5)**

ANNUAL OBJECTIVES

Album Sales: *The target for* Purple Rain *this year was 750,000 copies. Accounting is still finalizing the numbers, but it looks like we will beat that number by around ten million. Nice work. I would like to give you a higher score here, but remember that we are still quite a bit off the pace of* Thriller. **Score: (4/5)**

Movie Box Office Sales: *I know from prior conversations that you believe we didn't agree to a target for the film, but HR backs me up on this. We set the target at $65M, which coincidentally is right where the domestic gross is coming in. And while it may seem like a $65M movie with a budget of $7M should be very profitable, Accounting is quite certain that we will lose money on the picture (so don't expect any big royalty checks in the future!) Even if I could share all the cost details with you, I suspect it would be too difficult for* *you to fully understand.* **Score: (3/5)**

<u>Promotional Budget:</u> *Our budget for this year across the album and the movie was $2.5M. Instead, we spent in excess of $3M because of your numerous requests for additional support. Here at Warner Bros., we take budgeting very seriously. Where would this company be if everyone exceeded their promotional budget?* **Score: (2/5)**

SUMMARY

Average score on Success Factors: 3
Average score on Annual Objectives: 3
Final score: 3 (Meets Expectations)

I realize this score may be disappointing to you, Mr. Nelson, but please remember that you are still early in your career here at Warner Bros. With more time and additional focus on your development areas (teamwork, communication, meeting deadlines and staying within your promotional budget) you should easily exceed this score next year and put yourself solidly on track for promotion to senior assistant manager in the next several years.

Oh, and one more thing. It is my pleasure to inform you that your performance review score qualifies you for a significant bump in your base pay. Look for the additional

1.5% in your check starting in May.

Best regards,
Jack Pearson
Special Assistant VP, Urban Funk Music, Central Region
Warner Bros. Records

The Problems with Performance Management "Systems"

When companies are small, their leaders can observe everyone's performance firsthand. This intimacy makes it easy for managers to identify their best and worst employees. As firms grow, this becomes impossible, not because of management indifference, but because managers have too little direct exposure to many people in the organization.

Companies respond by implementing performance management "systems," which often involve standardized performance review paperwork that must be filled out on defined schedules. These reviews typically rate employees on five- or seven-point scales along a number of dimensions that some mysterious human resources (HR) committee has determined are most relevant.

As in our faux Prince review, ratings of personal characteristics (e.g., critical thinking, "presence", teamwork, etc.) are often paired with assessments of an employee's performance against objectives set at the beginning of the year. We are told these goals are desirable because they are "objective" and "measurable," relieving us of the risk that a biased or incompetent manager will stick us with an unfairly bad score. The reviewer merely has to check to see if the promised results were actually delivered. What could be simpler or more reasonable?

Objective measures sound great, but anyone who has been part of a corporate review process knows that the reality falls far short of the promise. Why does this happen?

Here is what every performance review gets wrong:

PROBLEM #1:

A person's contribution cannot be captured with a few metrics. We want everything to be measurable, but much of life is not, especially the things we value most. Consider, for example, how you would use a few metrics and a five-point scale to rate your mother's performance. Could you do so without failing to describe some of the most important things about her? What metrics would best reflect the impact she has had on your life? Would you give her a "4" on "job skills and knowledge?" How about a "3" on her annual objective of making you feel loved?

Employees are not family members, but great employees are special, and a simple form with a few metrics will never suffice in capturing their contribution. Amazing people are different in ways that can be difficult for us to articulate. Trying to do so leads to brilliance being sold short, the worst possible outcome for an organization.

PROBLEM #2:

Individual employees cannot accomplish much without good teammates and good luck. Companies are complex hives of people, where collaboration is required to do anything meaningful. Strangely, performance reviews do not acknowledge this reality. When determining if objectives are met, managers are not encouraged to think about the context. What if a great employee is stuck on a project with a bunch of mediocre teammates? How will she get credited for her outsized role? Will she get additional credit if she somehow manages to overcome her teammates' inertia?

And how should we account for good or bad luck? If someone inherits the dividends of her predecessors' smart decisions, should we not handicap her accomplishments somehow? If new market forces suddenly appear, damaging her business in ways she cannot reasonably prevent, should we reset her scores accordingly? If we did so, would this still be "objective?"

PROBLEM #3:

Goals can be easily manipulated, and they grow obsolete long before review time. Setting measurable objectives at the beginning of the year, a task that is viewed as critical to nearly every performance management scheme, is problematic for two reasons. The first, and by far the most insidious, is that employees have a strong incentive to "sandbag" by setting objectives that are very easy to accomplish. Managers are supposed to prevent this, but sometimes they are too lazy to enforce reasonable standards, and other times they are fooled by their direct reports, who often have information advantages because they are closer to the work. The end result is that unscrupulous employees achieve their objectives more often than others and win higher performance ratings at the end of the year. This is obviously a terrible outcome for the company.

The second issue with annual goal setting is that today's business environment is way too dynamic for strategies and priorities to survive unscathed for an entire year. Competitors introduce new products, customers develop new preferences, and governments pass new laws. Human Resources departments usually answer this objection by telling employees to renegotiate new objectives with their managers every time business conditions change. But that is unrealistic, and probably foolish. Imagine how much time we would all dedicate to this process if we had to reset objectives every time something material changed!

Setting goals is a good thing to do because it forces you to think strategically, to prioritize what is most important and to very carefully consider trade-offs. But using those goals as a scorecard in a performance review is naively simplistic. The world is much more complicated than that.

PROBLEM #4:

We think everybody is above average, but nobody is better than the rest of us. I once served on a senior committee that allowed me to see the performance management data for a company with a hundred thousand employees. Reviews were scored on a five-point scale, with "5" being best and "3" described as "meets expectations." The data showed that scores of "1" were non-existent. Ratings of "5" were uncommon too, except with a few managers who handed them out as freely as the stale coffee in the breakroom. This all translated into an average review score of 3.7 and an effective range of 2.7 to 4.2. The average score was well above average (3.7 instead of 3.0), and we were using a very small slice of the scale--five points had shrunk to one and a half!

This appears to happen in nearly every organization, and it comes from two deeply rooted aversions. First, none of us want to experience the pain of telling someone they are not good at something. Once we escape the barbarism of childhood, we grow to realize that the easiest way to avoid this unpleasantness is to tell a white lie. If a petite and uncoordinated friend asks us about their prospects for making the varsity basketball team, we look them straight in the eye and tell them that their crossover dribble alone will make them a lock. Similarly, if we have an employee who is struggling in their role, we write them up as average in their performance review. This is, unfortunately, the cruelest path we can take because it enables them to continue wasting their lives doing things they are not very good at. But it is easier on us, so we do it.

Second, few of us want to believe that one of our direct reports is more valuable than we are, or has more potential than we do. If we see some evidence to the contrary, our brains work furiously to find new proof of our employee's mediocrity. You will almost certainly doubt this claim, and you will imagine yourself to be completely innocent of anything like it, but this tendency is present in all of us. Ask yourself how many times you have given an employee a higher rating than the one you thought you deserved.

Fixing Performance Management[4]

March 10, 1985

To: Cliff Anderson, VP, Urban Funk Music, Central Region
From: Jack Pearson, Special Assistant VP, Urban Funk Music, Central Region
Re: Prince's Performance Review

Dear Cliff,

I gave Prince his performance review last week and I wanted to let you know that he didn't take the feedback very well.

We were discussing his scores in each performance category

---

[4] This pamphlet applies to most roles in an organization, but there are exceptions. Salespeople are quite different from most employees in that their contributions are often individual and tangible. Consequently, I would recommend keeping salespeople on high variable pay schemes that are a direct function of how much product/service they sell.

and I could see that he was starting to get agitated, but I really didn't think he would go as crazy as he did. He must have read ahead to the end of the review because just as I was reinforcing how important it is that we don't exceed our promotional budgets around here, he jumped out of his chair and grabbed the bowl of jellybeans on my desk and threw the whole damn thing on the floor, shattering the crystal into bits and scattering the candy all over my nice oak parquet. Then he began jumping up and down, smashing the beans here and there with his rhinestone-encrusted, high-heeled boots and yelling, "Three?! A three out of five?! You have to be f***ing kidding me!" And then he started stringing together even more expletives and talking about how many tens of millions of dollars he made for Warner Brothers and how we just didn't get it.

As you can imagine, I couldn't take that sitting down, so I stood up and pointed my finger at him and said, "Listen here young man, you're acting like you're something special around here! We all have to play by the rules, and that starts with defining clear, objective and measurable goals at the beginning of the year and then subjecting ourselves to an honest assessment twelve months later." And then I reminded him that I had coached many greats over the years, from Jermaine Jackson to Ray Parker Jr., and as brilliant as they all were, they didn't expect any special treatment, so he had better get used to it and fall into line.

That all must have really stung because he stormed out of my office while muttering something about the entire Warner executive team put together having less talent than what he has in his left buttock. Then he drop-kicked that large potted fern we have in the lobby, which I will remind you was a gift from Phil Specter. We are still trying to vacuum all the potting soil out of the carpet.

Anyway, just an FYI for you. I will handle it. I am going to bring HR into this and get him settled down. I will suggest we enroll him in some anger management seminars, and maybe some teamwork exercises with blindfolds and trust falls.

Best regards,
Jack Pearson
Special Assistant VP, Urban Funk Music, Central Region
Warner Bros. Records

The main objective of a performance management system should be to help an organization develop and retain its best people while pruning out its poorest performers. *The system's goal cannot be to make every employee better, nor can it be to ensure that the best employees get more compensation.*

Performance management systems almost always get this wrong. It is not hard to understand why. Improving every employee's performance is a romantic ideal that we all feel we should support. And paying a company's best performers more makes good, logical sense. *But pursuing these two objectives gets in the way of the more important goal: Increasing the organization's density of high performers.*

Why should we not try to help every employee improve? Because for somebody to improve, they must have the desire to improve, the ability to improve, and access to accurate feedback.

Who does not want to improve? Lots of people, unfortunately. Perhaps someone is too late in their career to think it is worth the effort to change. Or maybe they have been too successful and cannot believe that anything needs to change. Or perhaps they are just delusional and stubborn, a strikingly common combination in poor performers.

Other people want to improve but are not able to. This does not seem right to us. We are taught to believe that anyone can improve at anything. But can everyone, at any point in their career, become more creative? More charismatic? A better leader? And even if they could, would the gains be worth the investment required? A company might, with a lot of time and attention, marginally improve their worst employees on some of these dimensions, but would it not be better to just find people who are more naturally talented in these areas?

Even if people want to improve and are able to do so, they still need accurate feedback. Because our perceptions of ourselves are so optimistic, it is critical that we get honest, direct coaching about what we could be doing better. As we have discussed, managers rarely deliver such feedback because it is painful to do so.

The seemingly smart objective of using performance management systems to reward high performers with higher wages makes this problem worse. Now, in addition to feeling bad about hurting an employee's feelings, managers worry that they are affecting their colleagues' livelihoods. Instead of just relaying to Bill that he is a poor communicator who commands little respect from his colleagues, an intimidating enough task, the manager now has to tell Bill that his bonus and raise are much smaller than he expected.

Managers are supposed to be courageous enough to do this, to cut through whatever unease they might feel and do what is best for the company. But managers are human beings, and they will shrink from this duty in whatever way they can, in part because there is so little upside for them. Why suffer the "costs" of an angry, disengaged employee when it would be far less painful to tell Bill he is doing fine, give him a "meets expectations" on his performance review, and hope to nudge him into a different role in the firm, where he can be someone else's problem?

For all these reasons, performance management systems help slowly kill big companies. High performers do not get clear signals that they are valued, and low performers do not get direct feedback on where they are failing. Just as importantly, the company itself cannot identify its best and worst employees.

To fix performance management systems, some radical changes are needed. In this next section, I will explore five interrelated ideas for improving performance management in larger organizations:

1. Break the link between performance reviews and pay.
2. Make performance reviews qualitative and voluntary.
3. Reward excellence through promotion and recognition, *not* pay.
4. Identify candidates for promotion through forced ranking.
5. Fight title inflation through centralized rationing.

IDEA #1:

Break the link between performance reviews and pay. Many companies accept that they will have wide performance gaps between their best and worst employees in any particular position. To make this condition fairer, most firms try to pay their best employees more, using their performance management systems to determine who will get rewarded with higher salaries and bonuses. This sounds like a sound strategy, but it can often be harmful to the company.

Wide variations in pay for the "same job" can have serious consequences for morale, even if the highest compensation is perfectly matched to the best people.[5] Low performers will know

---

[5] You could reasonably argue great performers are not doing the "same job" as poor performers because they are creating more value for the firm, but let's set that aside for now.

they are getting paid much less than some of their peers. This will feel painfully unfair to them because of their distorted self-perception--remember, we all think we are above average. Their minds will scramble to find unjust causes outside of their control, like a bad boss, or jealous peer reviewers. And in many cases, their skepticism about the fairness of the performance management system will be justified.

In reality, companies are not very good at matching pay and performance. The problems often start at the beginning of the hiring process, when the firm makes offers to its final candidates. The initial salary presented is usually a direct function of what the candidates think they are "worth," or what they are currently being paid, both of which are poor predictors of how valuable someone will be at the new company. Furthermore, any increases to the offer will be driven by how aggressively the candidates negotiate. In the end, the highest rewards will flow to people with the best negotiating skills and greatest self-confidence, not necessarily to the best incoming candidates.

This initial pay disparity, with the highest salaries going to the most confident negotiators before an ounce of work has been done, often becomes a permanent feature of the company's compensation landscape. Nearly all future rewards, whether they are bonuses or salary increases, or sometimes even equity grants, will be calculated off this initial position. If Malcolm negotiates a 30% higher initial salary than Cassandra, he will enjoy roughly 30% more rewards than Cassandra during his time at the firm, even if he ends up being half the employee that she is.

A perfect performance management system would rectify this injustice, moving Malcolm's compensation down and Cassandra's up until they lined up perfectly with their contributions, but this almost never happens. As we have discussed, managers do not push their high performers and their low performers far enough apart in their review ratings, instead giving all their team members scores that range from average to above average. And even if they did give the best employees very high scores, and their worst performers very low ones, the range of acceptable salary increases the firm allows would often be too modest to restore proper balance.

A better system would reject wide compensation variation and instead pay everyone working a particular job the same salary (or a very tight range of salaries to accommodate peculiar circumstances.) For this approach to work, wide variations in performance between employees at the same level could not be allowed, otherwise the best employees would feel exploited. Instead, high performers would need to be publicly recognized and rewarded with promotions, while poor performers would have to be moved into less demanding roles or dismissed from the firm.

This kind of system would face the most internal resistance when the firm recruited new talent. Paying candidates their "market" wage would no longer be possible in all circumstances. The job would be offered at a consistent salary to everyone. Candidates with the highest current salaries, or the highest opinions of their self-worth, would probably reject the company's offers, which would cause many hiring managers to beg for exceptions to these rules. But I would argue that if losing great candidates is happening frequently, then the company is either 1) Paying too little compensation to the existing employees in the role or 2) Expecting too little from the people who are currently in the position. In either case, the firm's bigger problem is that it has a misalignment between the level of talent it wants and the compensation it is willing to pay. This problem needs to be addressed systematically, not with each individual hire.

With compensation standardized across all employees in a particular role, the link between pay and performance reviews would be broken. Both employers and employees would no longer demand, or even expect, that performance reviews would be used to allocate variable rewards, like bonuses and annual raises. *Breaking this link would be the critical first step in fixing performance management because it would increase the likelihood that feedback would be more honest and plentiful.*

IDEA #2:

Make performance reviews qualitative and voluntary. With performance reviews no longer used to determine pay raises and bonuses, companies could stop the absurd practice of trying to reduce their employees' contributions to a few numbers on a form.

Numbers in performance reviews are designed for two purposes and fail at both. The first is to promise the employee that this process is objective, that a biased manager will be constrained from delivering an unfair review. This is ridiculous, of course. An evil manager can always find ways to sabotage a direct report's review, either by setting impossible objectives, or by ignoring the employee's contributions. And besides, the process of assigning "objective" numbers to metrics can be easily manipulated--remember Prince's performance review?

The second reason numbers are used on performance reviews is to reassure employees that the spoils will be split fairly, that Cassandra's bonus will always be higher than Malcolm's if her review score exceeds his. This sounds perfectly fair and appropriate, but it makes two assumptions that cannot possibly be true: 1) That managers always assign the best scores to their best employees and 2) That different managers will somehow assign the same scores to the same level of performance--that Manager A's "4" will be the same as Manager B's "4." For these things to happen, human beings would need to be reliably reducible to numbers, and managers would have to be omniscient and flawless.

A better performance review would start with these assumptions and principles:

1. Assessing employee performance is a subjective craft, not an objective science. It will never be perfectly accurate or fair.
2. Words are better than numbers for describing employee performance.
3. The most important outcome of performance reviews is employee self-reflection.
4. Employees cannot get better without honest feedback.
5. Only some employees are ready to hear honest feedback.

The first three principles, if applied, require a radical overhaul to most performance review forms.

For our performance reviews at RISC, a non-profit I run with Steve Levitt, we eschew numbers and instead ask employees to write two essays that answer these simple questions:

1. What good things happened this year because of your efforts?
2. How did you make the people around you better?

After completing the essays, employees pass them up to their manager who reads them and appends their own comments. The review process then ends with an hour-long conversation where employees can ask clarifying questions and offer their thoughts on how they will improve next year.

Although many questions could work well in this process, we have chosen these two at RISC because they seem to solicit deep employee self-reflection on the dimensions we care most about. The first question's clause of, "because of your efforts" compels most people to describe *how* and *why* their efforts were critical to any successful initiatives. These details help both the manager and the employee understand whether the employee's contributions were unique and valuable, or whether they were just fortunate to be in the right place at the right time.

The second question about how the employee made the people around them better is unusual and sometimes jarring to our newest employees. Because most of us spend much of our life being graded for our individual efforts, especially in school, we often lose sight of what should be painfully obvious: That working for any organization comes with obligations outside of ourselves. Do we energize people with our presence in meetings? Do people want us on their teams because we are so reliable and pleasant to work with? Do we generously share credit with them when the team enjoys success? A great employee, through their optimism, their generosity, and their empathy, makes everyone around them better. Unfortunately, we have all seen examples of the opposite, where team members accomplish great things for themselves but wreak havoc on everyone around them.

Writing these performance review essays is difficult. It requires an employee to carefully assess their contributions to the initiatives and the team of people they are working with. Not everyone wants to do the work, so at RISC we make it optional.

Making performance reviews optional is blasphemous in traditional Human Resources circles. To do so would be considered a betrayal of the company's obligation to its employees. This attitude is well intended. It recognizes that every employee deserves to receive feedback on their performance (if they want it), and it acknowledges that most managers hate giving feedback and will look for ways to avoid it.

But the inconvenient truth that this attitude fails to consider is that many employees are not ready to hear or act on feedback. Changing habits and behaviors is extremely hard. It does not happen unless the person in question accepts that they need to change and commits to the unpleasant process of doing so. This is just as true for behaviors like "being present at meetings" or "supporting the team" as it is for losing weight or giving up scotch.

Going through the process of generating performance reviews for employees who do not want them is wasteful, consuming many hours of managerial time. The pointlessness of this exercise makes managers and employees resentful, increasing their cynicism about a process that should be viewed as revealing and helpful. This is one of the great tragedies of performance management systems.

But what about the managers? Don't they need to conduct performance reviews to understand how well each of their team members are doing? While it is possible for a review process to help a manager better understand an employee's strengths and weaknesses, especially if it includes a mechanism for gathering feedback from coworkers, it will rarely change their perception of how well an employee is performing. This may sound disturbing, but what is a performance review other than a distillation of the hundreds of observations a manager has made throughout the course of the year? Those observations have already informed the manager's current view. Managers are not surprised to learn that their best employee scores highly in the review process. Are teachers surprised that their best student has the highest grade at the end of the term?

As we will discuss in idea #4, every manager, at any given time, can identify who they believe are their best and worst employees. They do not need a performance review process to do so.

IDEA #3:

Reward excellence through promotion and recognition, not pay. In Idea #1 in this pamphlet, I advocated paying everyone in the same role the same salary. This approach has many benefits but one very large risk: The organization's best performers may lose their motivation as they realize they are doing better work than their peers for the same compensation.

The most effective way to hedge against this risk is to more quickly and frequently promote high performers into new positions with new titles. Titles are an effective (and often cheap!) way to slake employees' thirst for recognition. Titles also allow employees to clearly understand and signal their value within the organization, a very fundamental human need.[6]

Some of the world's largest and oldest organizations learned this lesson centuries ago. The US Army, for example, has 12 ranks for enlisted troops, five titles for warrant officers, and 11 ranks for commissioned officers.[7]

In addition to these formal ranks, the US Army has many other ways for soldiers and officers to earn recognition and signal their value, including service badges that display their specialized skills (e.g., combat medical, parachutist, etc.) to a multitude of medals and ribbons, ranging from the mundane (Cold War Medal) to the incredibly prestigious (Medal of Honor).[8]

---

[6] See Thorstein Veblen's *The Theory of the Leisure Class* for a discussion of the human need to signal one's value and standing to others. Veblen coined the term "conspicuous consumption." Today's "virtue signaling" is a derivative of this idea.

[7] https://www.army.mil/ranks/

[8] https://www.army.mil/uniforms/;
https://www.americanwarlibrary.com/display/usa.htm

Current Ranks in the US Army

Enlisted Ranks	Warrant Officer Ranks	Commissioned Officer Ranks
Private	Warrant Officer 1	Second Lieutenant
Private First Class	Chief Warrant Officer 2	First Lieutenant
Specialist	Chief Warrant Officer 3	Captain
Corporal	Chief Warrant Officer 4	Major
Sergeant	Chief Warrant Officer 5	Lieutenant Colonel
Staff Sergeant		Colonel
Sergeant First Class		Brigadier General
Master Sergeant		Major General
First Sergeant		Lieutenant General
Sergeant Major		General
Command Sergeant Major		General of the Army
Sergeant Major of the Army		

Source: https://army.mil/ranks.

You may think that armies are poor analogs for civilian organizations, but the US Army, with its 470,000 active-duty soldiers, has many of the same performance management challenges that Walmart has with its 2.2 million employees.[9] Most importantly, it has to find and reward its highest performing soldiers, and it has to do so without paying them big bonuses or disparate salaries.

The best objection to the concept of lots of titles, and the one that many HR executives will make, is that it can create fat and slow-moving organizations with unnecessary levels of management. This is often true, but it is only likely when a common norm is adopted: Everyone with a certain title must report to someone with the next highest title (e.g., all managers must report to directors.)

This norm makes good logical sense, and for organizations like the US Army, where titles are strongly linked to management scope (e.g., platoons are led by lieutenants, companies by captains, etc.), breaking this practice could be difficult, or even unwise. But for most organizations, titles do not need to be so tightly associated with the number of people an employee is managing, or the revenues of the business she is leading. If Janet is an exceptional leader who is greatly valued by the company, she should be given a prestigious title, even if she has few or no direct reports. *In other*

---

[9] https://www.statista.com/statistics/232330/us-military-force-numbers-by-service-branch-and-reserve-component/;
https://www.macrotrends.net/stocks/charts/WMT/walmart/number-of-employees

words, titles should signal an employee's value to the organization, not necessarily their scope of responsibility.

When titles are associated with scope, it tends to encourage two phenomena that are destructive to organizations. The first is a structural rigidity that does not flex to accommodate changes in talent. This most often takes the form of delayed or denied promotions for emerging superstars. For example, everyone may agree that Chris is a brilliant manager who is ready for promotion, but Chris is reminded that all the available director spots are filled and he must be patient. Given how rare top performers are, and how important it is for an organization to find and retain them, does this make any sense? Of course not. Chris will grow bitter as he waits, and should a headhunter call him anytime while he is in his promotion purgatory, he will be tempted to leave.

The second damaging phenomenon caused by tying titles to scope is empire building. Striving employees, recognizing that someone's "span of control" is highly correlated to their title, will aggressively seek to acquire new areas of responsibility and hold on to the ones they have. In some cases, this is fine, or even good, but in most environments this causes pain and inefficiency, with executives leading areas they are not well equipped to handle.

If an organization releases itself from the conventional wisdom, allowing titles to have varying spans of control and reporting relationships, *it can use title promotion as its main means of rewarding high performers AND maintain a flat organization.*

As Figure 7 shows, it is quite easy to draw up an organizational chart with eight different titles but only four layers of management, bracketed by an SVP and an entry-level analyst.

The best argument against numerous titles in an organization is the fear of title inflation. Without strong controls, managers will want to reward their best or most loyal employees with frequent promotions, some of which will be unwarranted. Tying titles to spans of control is one way of fighting this tendency, but as we have discussed, it comes at the cost of organizational flexibility and the risk of losing the company's best talent. Idea #5 will offer a better way to mitigate the risk of title inflation.

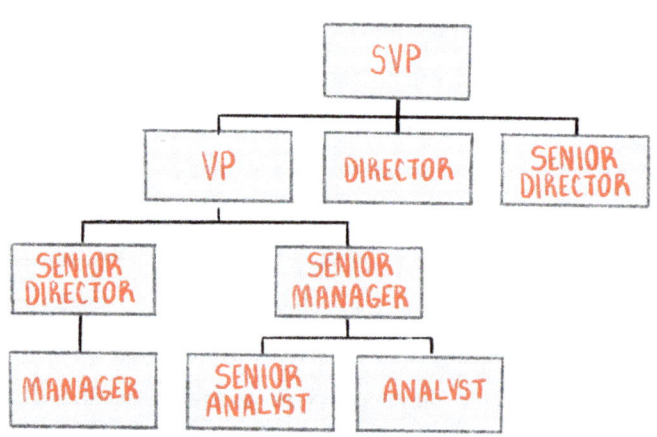

FIGURE 7

IDEA #4:

Identify candidates for promotion through forced ranking.

If an organization's best performers are rewarded through promotion, and performance reviews are qualitative and voluntary, managers will need a method for determining who is most deserving of the next promotion.

Let us imagine that we were the mythical "Jack Pearson" who authored Prince's 1984 performance review at the beginning of this chapter. If the CEO of Warner Brothers called us sometime in 1985 and asked us to choose only two artists from our portfolio to "promote," how would we go about deciding who to put forward?

The conventional HR wisdom would have us pull out Prince's performance review and compare his scores to the other artists on our roster (let us assume our roster, in addition to Prince, included Ray Parker Jr., Whitney Houston, Michael Jackson, Cyndi Lauper, Huey Lewis, Tina Turner, and Sting.) But would we really do that? Would we really trust that those scores were a reflection of the ground truth about the artists' performance and potential? Or would we be more inclined to believe that the numbers on the forms were subject to some amount of error and chance?

I believe we would distrust whatever was written in the performance reviews and instead arrange the artists in a forced rank list, using our intuitions. My prioritized list would have looked like this:

1. Michael Jackson
2. Prince
3. Tina Turner
4. Sting
5. Whitney Houston
6. Cyndi Lauper
7. Huey Lewis
8. Ray Parker Jr.

How different would your list have been back in 1985? I am guessing we all would have agreed on who should be #1 and #8. Ray Parker Jr. had a big hit with his theme song for *Ghostbusters* in 1984, but we probably would have been skeptical that he could compete in the long run with this very talented group. And Michael Jackson, three years post *Thriller*, was well established as the "King of Pop."

Agreeing on the rankings between #2 and #7 would have been more difficult, but I am certain we could have reached a consensus. Could many people have reasonably argued that Huey Lewis should be ahead of Tina Turner? Or that Cyndi Lauper should have outranked Prince?

How would we have come to an agreement? Would we have referred back to Whitney Houston's objectives in 1984 to make sure that she had stayed within her promotional budget? Would we have checked Sting's "Teamwork" score to see if he had been scored higher than a "3?" Of course not. Instead, we would have built our consensus by having a conversation. We would have gathered around a conference table, real or virtual, and would have debated each artist's merits, using the hundreds of bits of information we had through our collective observations and experiences with this group.

But would that be fair? What if our views did not accurately represent a particular artist? What if you disliked Tina Turner because you thought she should have left Ike sooner? What if I objected to Sting's haircut? If either of us changed our rankings because of these meaningless impressions, that would certainly be unfair. But the myth that we have all been sold is that this is somehow avoidable, that a performance review form with "measurable" objectives and "quantifiable" metrics somehow relieves us of the imprecision of human beings judging other human beings. *The process of assessing people is never perfectly fair*.

This ranked list of artists, once established, would be relatively easy to update. Human performance changes over time, of course, but rankings relative to peers do not shift abruptly or frequently. As the 1980s progressed, Sting and Whitney Houston may have moved up this list a bit, while Cyndi Lauper and Huey Lewis may have faded. If we had gathered every six months to review our artist rankings, we could have come to an agreement on a revised list in pretty short order.

What works for pop stars at a record label can work for engineers at a technology company. Managers can meet every six months, or even as infrequently as once a year, to develop a consensus on a ranked list of employees who are working in the same roles. Once established, this list can serve as the central guide for determining who will be promoted next in the organization.

Forced ranking makes many people uncomfortable. Much of this discomfort, as we have previously discussed, comes from our aversion to telling anyone that they are doing poorly. Another source of unease is our common belief that all *our* team members are above average, in the same way that most people dislike the US Senate but love their own state's senators. These objections are irrational tics of sorts, rooted deeply in our human psychology.[10]

A more rational grievance against forced ranking can be found in its tendency to overemphasize meaningless differences. While it was clear that Michael Jackson was a far better pop star than Ray Parker Jr., it was much less obvious that Tina Turner was better than Sting. What possible good could come from telling Sting that he was one spot behind Tina in the rankings? Similarly, it is not helpful for an employee at a tech company to know that he is the 17th best engineer in a pool of thirty. That precision is both false and unhelpful. He may easily spend too much time worrying about who was ranked 16th and 18th instead of thinking about the key takeaway for him: His company views him as an average engineer.

There are two groups of people who need to know precisely where they are in any forced ranking: the very high and very low

---

[10] I often call this the Lake Wobegon Effect, after the line in Garrison Keilor's *A Prairie Home Companion*, "Welcome to Lake Wobegon, where all the women are strong, all the men are good-looking, and all the children are above average." Psychologists refer to this phenomenon as illusory superiority: https://en.wikipedia.org/wiki/Illusory_superiority

performers. Superstars need to understand they are highly valued and will be rewarded with an imminent promotion so that they do not get tempted away by another opportunity. And employees who are struggling, or who just have the misfortune of being outclassed by their peers, need to know that they are in the back of the pack. Disclosing this is not cruel, as many of us tend to feel. In fact, it is quite the opposite. Choosing *not* to disclose this is cruel because it allows people to continue wasting time in roles they are unlikely to ever succeed in. Armed with the knowledge that they are lagging, they can either rededicate themselves to improving, or they can start looking for a job that is better suited to their strengths.[11]

The perfect forced ranking system may look something like what I experienced as a student at Harvard's business school (HBS). At HBS, every professor, for every class, had to identify the top 15% and the bottom 10% of their students. The top performers received a grade of "I" and the laggards were given a "III." The middle 75% were granted a "II." A class with 60 students would look like this:

HBS Class of 60 students
Grade I   9 students
Grade II   45 students
Grade III 6 students

---

[11] This notion, that avoiding an honest discussion with poor performers was cruel because it allowed people to waste their lives, was first introduced to me in 1995 by Michael B. Jensen, a professor at Harvard Business School.

This HBS grading system elegantly accomplished the necessary outcomes we have been discussing in this fourth idea. The top students and the struggling students received clear signals of where they were at in the class so that they could make smarter decisions (Grade I students could either continue pressing and qualify for academic honors, or ease up a bit and get back some sleep and leisure time; Grade III students had to confront their poor performance and redouble their efforts, or perhaps consider withdrawing and studying something they were better suited for,) while the rest of the students, those with a Grade II, knew they were comfortably somewhere in the middle.

Any large organization could copy this kind of scheme for a forced ranking system.[12] If it did so, it could eliminate its current performance review forms, with their false objectivity and precision, and deliver better information to the employees it most needs to act on. The best employees would stay longer, and the worst employees would leave more quickly. The organization's density of high performers, our ultimate goal, would go up.

---

[12] Forced curves work best with large populations (20 or more.) If you have only three managers, you obviously cannot define the best 15%. Also, the smaller the population, the more legitimate the possibility that everybody is indeed good, or at least average. When the population is too small, you should simply identify the best and the worst employee. You may also consider merging the group with others doing very similar work until your population is large enough.

IDEA #5:

Fight title inflation through centralized rationing. As we discussed earlier, title inflation is a natural phenomenon that every organization has to fight against. Left unchecked, a higher and higher fraction of promotions will go to undeserving people. This happens for at least four reasons:

1. It feels good to tell people they are great. In the same way we seek to avoid sharing bad feedback with our coworkers, we take pleasure in praising and rewarding others.
2. Most of us believe our people are better than they are. The same lenses that distort our perceptions of our own abilities color our view of the people on our teams.
3. Promotions can serve as catnip for talent. Managers that promote people frequently are attractive to employees who are seeking advancement. These managers, like "easy A" professors at universities, will be popular and advantaged in the internal wars for talent.
4. Managers with more high-ranking people on their team are often perceived as having more power and prestige. Consequently, by promoting their employees, managers make it more likely that they themselves will be promoted.

All these perceptions and incentives nudge managers towards making too many promotions. But why should we care if promotions happen so easily? Have I not spent most of this pamphlet arguing that we should hand out more titles to more people?

The problem, of course, is not with how many promotions are made, but to whom they are given. All employees enjoy seeing their best-performing colleagues get rewarded. It is only when less-deserving coworkers get the spoils that resentment emerges, in the same way that we all get angry when someone cuts into a long line we are standing in at a store.

Because managers are inclined to give promotions to the wrong people, and because doing so is so destructive to the collective sense of fairness, organizations need a strong system for ensuring that promotions are awarded accurately. Such a system would start by trusting no single person, not even the CEO, to determine who gets a promotion. Decisions about promotions should instead be entrusted to committees.

I am typically very suspicious of committees, but in this case, they are the most appropriate mechanism for safeguarding promotional fairness.[13] Organizations should form committees for each level of potential promotion (manager, director, VP, etc.), composed of three leaders who sit two levels higher in the organization (i.e., directors should preside over decisions to promote analysts to managers.) Managers who want to promote

---

[13] Brad Anderson, the former CEO of Best Buy and a mentor of mine, claims that "nothing good has ever come out of a committee." I generally agree with this sentiment, especially with respect to innovation--a topic we will explore in another pamphlet. However, when it comes to making judgments about people, a small committee can help ensure some amount of accuracy and fairness, not unlike a judicial panel.

someone on their team should have to convince the committee. Cases involving employees who are not at the top of the forced ranking for their peer group (Idea #4) should be summarily rejected, or at least viewed with extreme skepticism.

Decision-makers on these committees need to be powerful enough to feel comfortable rejecting the requests that come before them. In a public company, these committees should report to the board of directors, and the board itself should be approving all officer promotions. *Boards should view the accuracy of promotions as a responsibility as sacred as any other they hold.*

In Sum

March 12, 1985

To: Jack Pearson, Special Assistant VP, Urban Funk Music, Central Region
From: Cliff Anderson, VP, Urban Funk Music, Central Region
Re: Prince's Performance Review

Dear Jack,

Thank you for the update on your performance review with Prince.

When you've been in the business as long as I have, you don't get surprised anymore. I have been dealing with these prima donna artists for decades now, and they're all the same. You just have to be firm with them, otherwise they will run roughshod over everyone. One of my proudest moments was when I was managing James Brown over at King Records in the early seventies. That man thought he was so special! He wouldn't take any feedback! We had several helpful suggestions for him about his hair, his shoes, his dance moves, etc. and he wouldn't listen to any of them! He told me that a white guy named Cliff from Council Bluffs, Iowa can't possibly know anything about funk. I was insulted, of course, and I reminded him that King Records had great confidence in my funk leadership, otherwise they would not have made me assistant manager of the Northwest Region. Finally, after walking on eggshells with him for months, I put my foot down over his management of his band. I told him it was unfair to have such high expectations of the brass section, and that if he wanted to continue to be a King Records man, he needed to lay off. Well, you would have thought I insulted his mother! He stormed out of the studio and signed a contract with Polydor the next day.

It's true that we lost a pretty good revenue stream that day, but I was proud that we preserved the culture of King Records.

Prince will have to learn how to be a team player. We can't afford to have him off doing his own thing, not involving management in his productions, and not actively participating in our weekly meetings. And exceeding his promotional budget is a red line he cannot cross again.

If Prince gets so upset that we lose him, don't worry about it. I don't think he has many songs left in him.

Best regards,
Cliff Anderson
VP of Urban Funk Music, Central Region
Warner Bros. Records

The argument I am making in this pamphlet can be summarized as follows:

- Most performance reviews are fatally flawed.
    - A review's metrics cannot fully capture a person's contribution.
    - Reviews do not account for the effects of good luck.
    - Reviews' "objective" measures can be easily manipulated.
    - Reviewers' incentives and psychology distort the assessments.

- These flaws slowly kill companies because high performers do not get clear signals that they are valued, and low performers do not get direct feedback on where they are failing. Just as importantly, the company itself cannot identify its best and worst employees.
- The main objective of a performance management system should be to help a company increase its density of high performers.
- Companies need to concentrate their development time and resources on employees who 1) Want to improve 2) Are capable of improving. Consequently, performance reviews should not be mandatory for every employee.
- Compensation should be decoupled from performance reviews, and great performance should be rewarded through promotion, not additional pay.
- Promotions should be determined through forced ranking of employees and approved by a select committee that reports to the board of directors.

If your company were to adopt the ideas presented in this chapter, performance management would change along nearly every meaningful dimension:

	Conventional Wisdom	**A Better Way**
The objective(s) of performance reviews are to . . .	Help every employee improve; ensure the best employees get higher compensation	Increase the organization's density of high performers
Do performance reviews affect compensation?	Yes	No
Does every employee need to receive a performance review?	Yes	No
A good performance review . . .	Is "objective" and numerical	Is qualitative and descriptive
Performance reviews are initiated by . . .	Managers	Employees

Great performance is rewarded primarily through . . .	Higher pay and bonuses	Promotion and recognition
Titles are . . .	Limited and tied to scope ("span of control")	Diverse and tied to the employee's value to the organization
Employees' rankings relative to peers are . . .	Unknown or arbitrary	Systematic and based on collective forced ranking
High performers and low performers . . .	Do not know how they rank versus their peers	Are given clear signals of their relative rank
Promotion decisions are made by . . .	Individual leaders or ad hoc processes	Formal committees of senior leaders, reporting up to the board of directors

ACKNOWLEDGEMENTS

I am grateful to several friends for their help on this project. Brad Anderson, who has long been a friend and a mentor to me, nudged me into putting my thoughts to paper. He also significantly influenced many of the ideas in this pamphlet, through both his leadership at Best Buy and our frequent, long discussions on the nature of organizations. Steve Levitt, my friend and current colleague, reminded me that, "nobody reads books anymore" and suggested I find other ways of illustrating my ideas. His skepticism caused me to abandon a book format and focus instead on delivering a series of pamphlets. Ahna Severts, my wife, patiently listened to hundreds of my rants and speculations and helped me to improve my thinking in every way—as she always does! Mara Severts, my daughter and budding artist, designed the cover and all the graphics. And several of my friends read my first drafts and offered helpful advice, including Dan Bauer, Dave Bryla, Jude Buckley, Scott Friesen, Leslie Lancry, Scott Moore, Jeff Nosbush, and JW Penland.

www.ingramcontent.com/pod-product-compliance
Lightning Source LLC
Chambersburg PA
CBHW070124230526
45472CB00004B/1404